By Ruth Owen

WINDMILL BOOKS

Published in 2023 by Windmill Books,
an Imprint of Rosen Publishing
29 East 21st Street, New York, NY 10010

Produced for Rosen by Ruth Owen Books

Designer
Emma Randall

Photos courtesy of Ruth Owen Books and Shutterstock

Cataloging-in-Publication Data
Names: Owen, Ruth.
Title: Get baking for Halloween! / Ruth Owen.
Description: New York : Windmill Publishing, 2023. | Series: Get baking for the holidays | Includes glossary and index.
Identifiers: ISBN 9781508198284 (pbk.) | ISBN 9781508198307 (library bound) | ISBN 9781508198291 (6pack) | ISBN 9781508198314 (ebook)
Subjects: LCSH: Halloween cooking--Juvenile literature. | Baking--Juvenile literature.
Classification: LCC TX739.2.H34 O944 2023 | DDC 641.5'68--dc23

Printed in the United States of America

CPSIA Compliance Information: Batch CSWM23: For Further Information contact Rosen Publishing, New York, New York at 1-800-237-9932

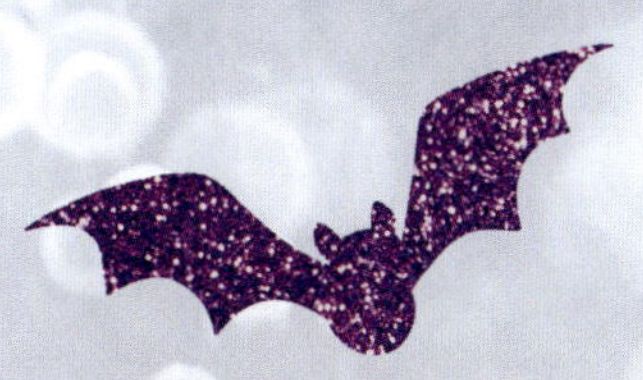

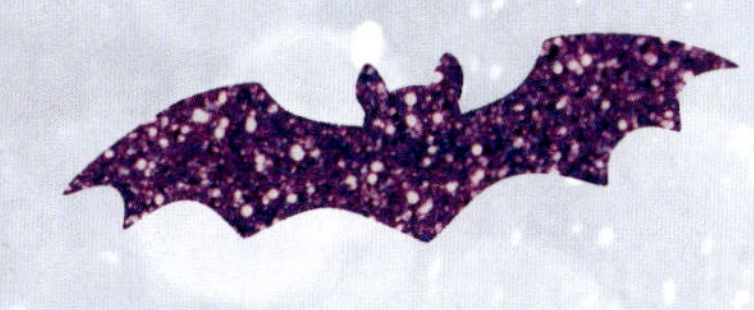

Contents

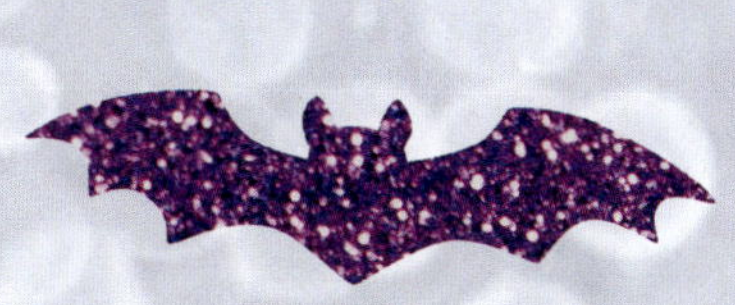

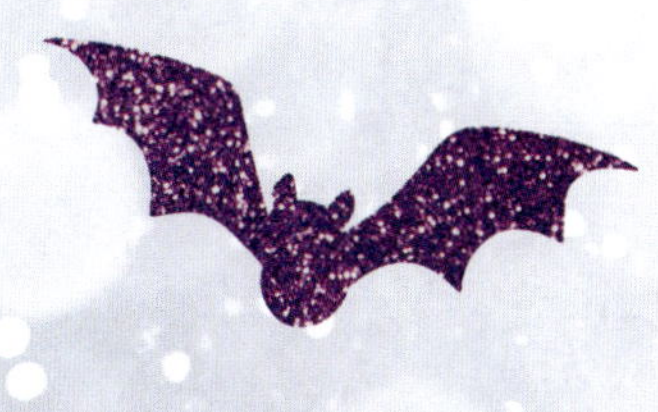

Get Ready to Bake

When Halloween comes around, it's the perfect opportunity to head to the kitchen and get baking.

Halloween is always more fun with friends. So invite some friends over and get baking together!

Measuring Counts

- Make sure you measure your ingredients carefully. If you get a measurement wrong, it could affect how successful your baking is.
- Use measuring scales or a measuring cup to measure dry and liquid ingredients.
- Measuring spoons can be used to measure small amounts of ingredients.

Be Prepared

- Before cooking, always wash your hands well with soap and hot water.
- Make sure the kitchen countertop and all your equipment is clean.
- Read the recipe carefully before you start cooking. If you don't understand a step, ask an adult to help you.
- Gather together all the ingredients and equipment you will need. Baking is more fun when you're prepared!

Have Fun, Stay Safe!

It's very important to have an adult around whenever you do any of the following tasks in the kitchen:

- Using a mixer, the stovetop burners, or an oven.
- Using sharp utensils, such as knives and vegetable peelers or corers.
- Working with heated pans, pots, or baking sheets.
- Always use oven mitts when handling heated pans, pots, or baking sheets.

REMEMBER:
Clean up the kitchen and put all your equipment away once you've finished baking.

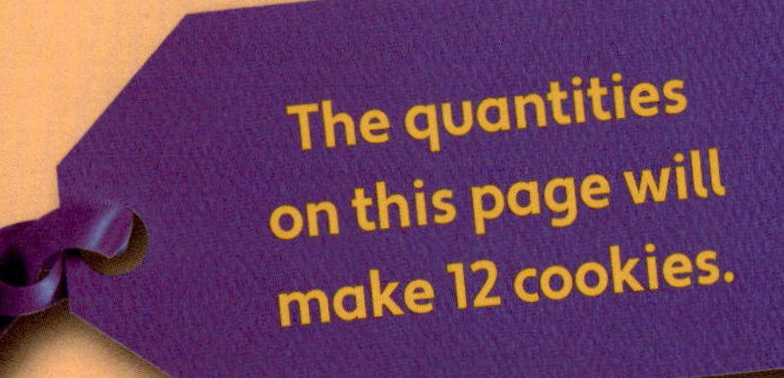

Ingredients

To make the cookie dough:

- 1 ½ cups all-purpose flour (plus a little extra for dusting)
- ½ cup powdered sugar
- 5 ounces butter or margarine (plus a little for greasing)
- 1 orange

To make the filling:

- 3 ½ ounces mascarpone cheese
- 1 teaspoon powdered sugar
- 1 heaping tablespoon semisweet chocolate chips

To make the glaze:

- ½ cup powdered sugar
- 1 tablespoon orange juice

Equipment

- 2 large cookie sheets
- Mixing bowl
- Wooden spoon
- Grater
- Plastic wrap
- Rolling pin
- 3-inch (8-cm) round cookie cutter
- Small, sharp knife
- Oven mitt
- Heatproof bowl
- Small saucepan
- Small dish
- Brush

Fruity Jack-o'-Lantern Treats

These jack-o'-lantern cookies are made with fruity **dough.** They are filled with chocolate-cheese frosting and have a sticky **glaze.** What a sweet treat! They are just perfect to share with your friends on Halloween after trick-or-treating.

Step 1 Grease the cookie sheets with a little butter to keep your cookies from sticking to the sheets.

Step 2 Put the butter and sugar into the mixing bowl and **beat** with a wooden spoon until smooth and fluffy.

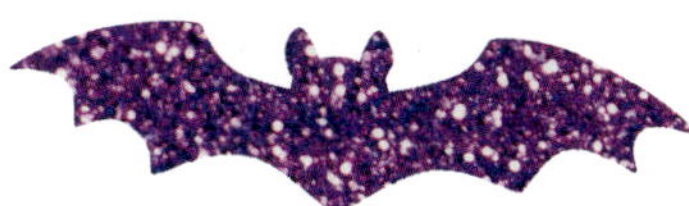

Step 3 Wash the orange and finely grate its rind to get **zest**. Cut the orange in half and squeeze the juice out in a bowl.

Step 4 Add the flour and orange zest to the bowl and beat the mixture until the ingredients are blended and become crumbly. Next, use your hands to squeeze and **knead** the mixture to make a ball of soft dough.

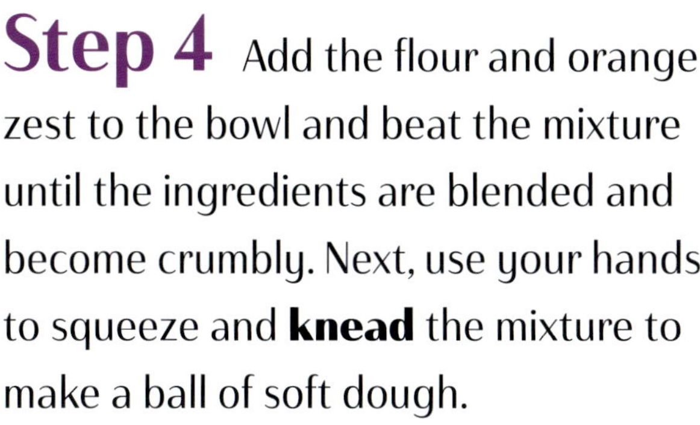

Step 5 Wrap the dough in plastic wrap and place in a refrigerator for one hour.

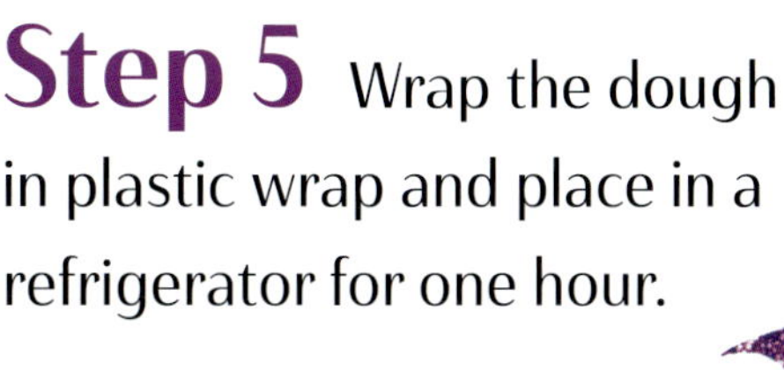

Step 6 **Preheat** the oven to 350°F (180°C).

Step 7 Dust your countertop with a little flour. Unwrap the dough and place it on the dusted surface. Roll out the dough to about a quarter of an inch (0.5 cm) thick.

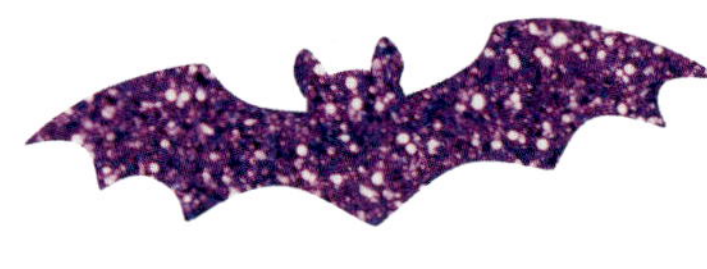

Step 8 Cut 24 circles from the dough and place them on the cookie sheets.

Step 9 On 12 of the circles (the front halves of the cookies) cut the eyes, nose, and mouth of a jack-o'-lantern. Using the blunt edge of your knife, make lines down the faces, too. Shape small pieces of dough into stalks and press them onto the faces.

The remaining 12 circles will form the back halves of the cookies.

Step 10 Bake the cookies for about 15 minutes, or until they are turning golden. Remove the cookies from the oven using an oven mitt and allow to cool completely.

Step 11 To make the filling, beat the powdered sugar and mascarpone cheese until they are creamy and smooth.

Step 12 Put the chocolate chips into the heatproof bowl. Add about 1 inch (2.5 cm) of water to the saucepan and set the bowl in the saucepan. Heat the saucepan on a medium heat, stirring the chocolate until it melts.

How to melt chocolate

Step 13 Wearing an oven mitt, remove the bowl from the saucepan. Allow the melted chocolate to cool for about 5 minutes. Then add the chocolate to the mascarpone and sugar and mix thoroughly.

The mixture should be a **consistency** similar to peanut butter.

Step 14 To make the glaze, mix the powdered sugar and orange juice until smooth and shiny.

Step 15 Spread some filling onto each of the plain cookie halves. Paint a thin layer of glaze over each face. Allow the glaze to dry, and then squash the two halves of each cookie together. Enjoy!

Frankenstein Cupcakes

These gruesomely green cakes are decorated to look like the face of Dr. Frankenstein's slow-moving, groaning monster from the old horror movies. Bake up a batch of delicious cupcakes, then carve out the monster faces and have fun "drawing" your monsters' hair, eyes, and other features using frosting and marshmallows.

The quantities on this page will make 12 cupcakes.

Ingredients

To make the cupcake batter:

- 7 ounces butter or margarine
- 1 cup superfine sugar
- 2 cups cake flour
- 1 teaspoon baking powder
- ¼ teaspoon salt
- 3 large eggs
- ½ teaspoon vanilla extract
- ½ cup milk

For the decorations and frosting:

- 3 cups powdered sugar
- 6 tablespoons milk
- Green food coloring
- 36 white mini marshmallows
- Tube of black frosting (with a nozzle for piping)

Step 1 Preheat the oven to 350°F (180°C).

Step 2 Line the muffin pan with the muffin cases.

Step 3 Put the butter and sugar into the mixing bowl and **cream together** with a wooden spoon until fluffy. If you wish, you can use an electric mixer for this step.

Step 4 Add the flour, baking powder, salt, eggs, vanilla extract, and milk. Use a wooden spoon or electric mixer to beat the ingredients together until the mixture is thick and smooth.

Equipment

- 12-hole muffin pan
- 12 muffin cases
- Mixing bowl
- Wooden spoon
- Electric mixer (optional)
- Oven mitt
- Potholder
- Metal skewer
- Wire rack for cooling
- Small serrated knife
- Small bowl
- Spoon
- Scissors

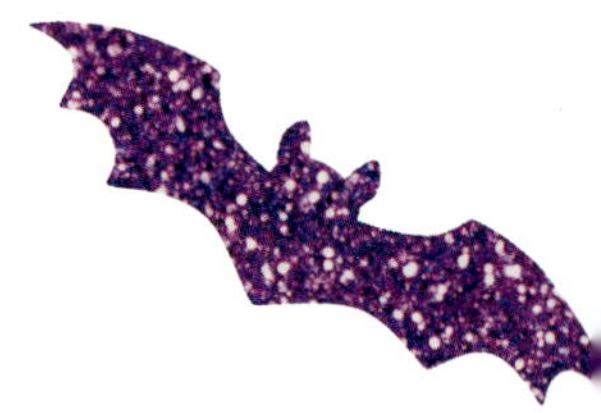

Step 5 Spoon the mixture into the muffin cases, dividing it equally.

Step 6 Bake the cakes for 20 minutes, or until they are golden and have risen above the edges of the muffin cases. To test if the cakes are baked, insert a metal skewer into one cake. If it comes out clean, the cakes are ready.

Step 7 Place the muffin pan on a potholder for about 5 minutes to cool. Then carefully place each cake on the wire rack and allow to cool completely.

Step 8 To carve the monster's face, carefully cut a small semicircle from each side of the cake with a serrated knife.

Step 9 Next, slice off any raised part of the cake to create a flat surface. Then cut down into this surface and carve off a thin slice to create the raised forehead and face.

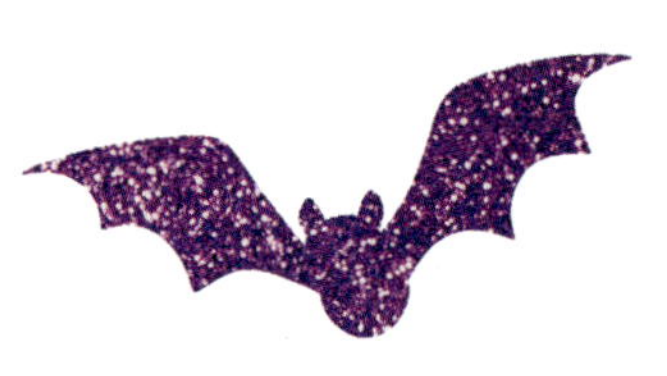

Step 10 Mix the powdered sugar, milk, and green food coloring to make the frosting. Add the green coloring in small drops. You can always add more, but you can't remove coloring once it's in the mixture!

The frosting should be smooth and thick, and slowly run off the spoon. If it's too thin or too thick, add more sugar or milk.

Step 11 Slowly **drizzle** the frosting over the cakes and allow it to flow over the faces. Add more frosting as needed and help smooth it into place with the spoon.

Put the cakes into the refrigerator for about 15 minutes to help the frosting set.

Step 12 Use two marshmallows to be the bolts on the monster's neck. Cut one marshmallow in half to make the white parts of its eyes.

Step 13 Use the black frosting to create the monster's hair, eyebrows, pupils, nose, and mouth.

Jack-o-Lantern Cupcakes

Carving a jack-o-lantern is an essential part of our Halloween preparations. But this year you can use your baking and decorating skills to create these pumpkin-shaped cupcakes with grimacing, toothy grins.

The quantities on this page will make 6 cupcakes.

Ingredients

To make the cupcake batter:

- 7 ounces butter or margarine
- 1 cup superfine sugar
- 2 cups cake flour
- 1 teaspoon baking powder
- ¼ teaspoon salt
- 3 large eggs
- ½ teaspoon vanilla extract
- ½ cup milk
- Orange food coloring

For the decorations and frosting:

- 1¼ cups powdered sugar
- 1 cup butter (tightly packed)
- 2 tablespoons milk
- Orange and green food coloring
- Mini white marshmallows
- Tube of black frosting

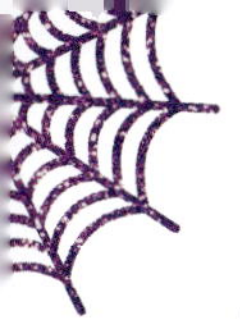

Step 1 Preheat the oven to 350°F (180°C).

Step 2 Line the muffin pan with the muffin cases.

Step 3 Put the butter and sugar into the mixing bowl and cream together with a wooden spoon until fluffy. If you wish, you can use an electric mixer for this step.

Step 4 Add the flour, baking powder, salt, eggs, vanilla extract, and milk. Use a wooden spoon or electric mixer to beat the ingredients together until the mixture is thick and smooth.

Step 5 Mix drops of orange food coloring into the cake batter until you have a pumpkin-like color.

Step 6 Spoon the mixture into the muffin cases, dividing it equally.

Equipment

- 6-hole muffin pan
- 6 muffin cases
- Mixing bowl
- Wooden spoon
- Electric mixer (optional)
- Oven mitt
- Potholder
- Metal skewer
- Wire rack for cooling
- 2 small dishes
- 2 spoons
- Small serrated knife
- Icing syringe (optional)
- Scissors

Step 7 Bake the cakes for 20–25 minutes. To test if the cakes are baked, insert a metal skewer into one cake. If it comes out clean, the cakes are ready.

Step 8 Place the cakes on a wire rack and allow to cool completely.

Step 9 To make the frosting, mix the powdered sugar, butter, and milk until it is thick and smooth. Put a couple of small spoonfuls into a separate dish.

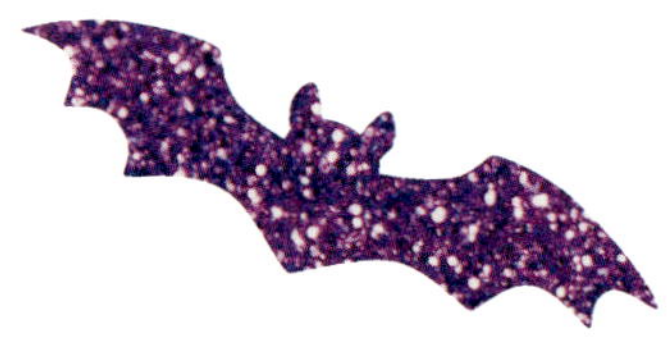

Step 10 Add orange food coloring to the bigger quantity of frosting, and green coloring to the smaller quantity.

Step 11 To make one jack-o'-lantern, take two cakes and carefully slice off the rounded tops with a serrated knife.

Step 12 Spread orange frosting on top of one cake. Then turn the other cake upside down and put it on top of the frosting.

Green frosting

Step 13 Using an icing syringe (or a spoon), add some green frosting to the top of the cake.

Use the black frosting to draw on eyes and a nose.

Icing syringe

Step 14 Carefully cut triangular teeth from the marshmallows and press them into the frosting.

You can add some green sprinkles, too.

Enjoy!

Mummy Bites

Get wrapping some sausages in dough bandages to create these not-so-scary Halloween mummies. They are super-quick to put together as all you need to make the wrappings is a tube of dough for crescent rolls.

The quantities on this page will make 12 to 24 mummies.

Ingredients

- 12 precooked sausages (or 24 cocktail sausages)
- 1 can of crescent roll dough (enough to make 6 rolls)
- 1 tablespoon honey
- 1 tablespoon ketchup
- 2 slices of any white cheese
- Mustard
- 3 black olives
- Cooking oil or spray for greasing

Step 1 Preheat the oven to 350°F (180°C).

Step 2 Brush or spray the baking pan with a little oil. This will keep your mummies from sticking to the pan.

Step 3 In a small bowl, mix the ketchup and honey together.

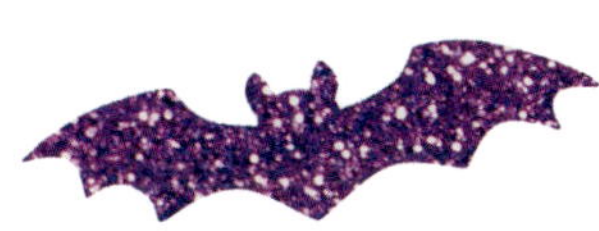

Step 4 Use the brush to cover the sausages in a light coating of the ketchup and honey mixture.

Equipment

- Baking pan
- 2 brushes
- Small bowl
- Spoon
- Small sharp knife
- Oven mitt
- Potholder
- Scissors

Step 5 Open the can of dough mix. Gently unroll the dough. A can with enough dough for six crescent rolls will contain three rectangles of dough.

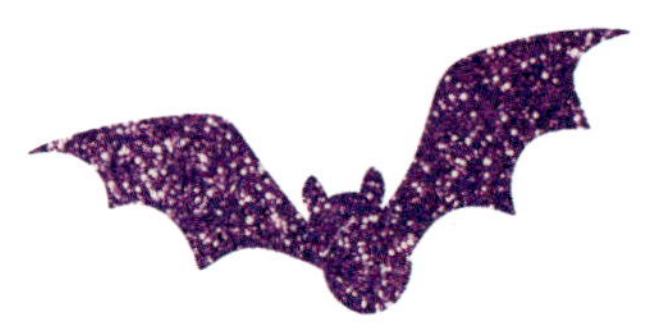

Step 6 Take one rectangle, and with your fingers, squeeze together the diagonal **perforations** to make a smooth rectangle of dough.

Next, carefully cut the dough into strips. Each strip should be about half an inch (1 cm) wide.

Step 7 Take one strip and start to wrap it around a sausage.

The ends of the strip will stick to the ketchup and honey mixture. Add a second strip of dough if needed. Leave an open space for the mummy's eyes.

Step 8 Place the mummies onto the baking pan and bake for 20 minutes. The mummies are ready when the dough bandages have turned a golden brown color.

Step 9 Using an oven mitt, carefully take the baking pan from the oven. Set the pan on a potholder to allow the mummies to cool.

Step 10 Cut tiny circles from the cheese slices and use a tiny blob of mustard to stick them to the mummies. Then cut tiny pieces of black olive (as pupils) and place one piece on each cheese circle.

Step 11 Your sausage mummies are ready to eat. Serve them drizzled with ketchup for a gory, bloody effect!

Spicy Halloween Apples

Sweet, spicy, and healthy, these baked apples with blackberries can be served with whipped cream or ice cream. They are a fantastic, warming dessert for a chilly October night.

The quantities on this page will make 4 baked apples.

Ingredients

- 4 Granny Smith or other cooking apples
- 4 tablespoons honey
- ½ teaspoon cinnamon
- 1 large orange
- 2 cups blackberries (fresh or frozen)

Step 1 Preheat the oven to 350°F (180°C).

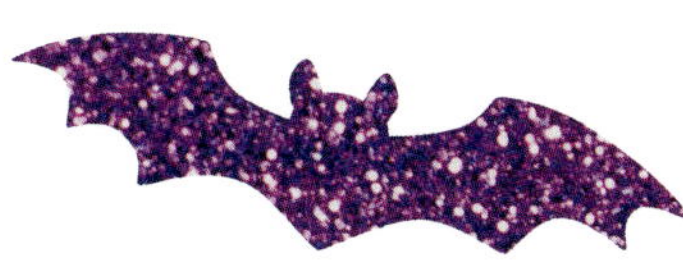

Step 2 Wash the apples and blackberries thoroughly. Wash the orange's skin, too.

Step 3 Carefully core the apples, leaving a hole just a little bigger than a quarter.

Next, carefully make a cut around the center of each apple, just cutting through the skin.

Step 4 Set the four apples in the foil dish or baking pan.

Equipment

- Apple corer
- Knife and chopping board
- Small foil dish or shallow baking pan
- Grater
- Hand juicer
- Small dish
- Spoon
- Oven mitt
- Potholder

Step 5 Finely grate the orange's rind. Then cut the orange in half and squeeze out all its juice with a hand juicer.

Hand juicer

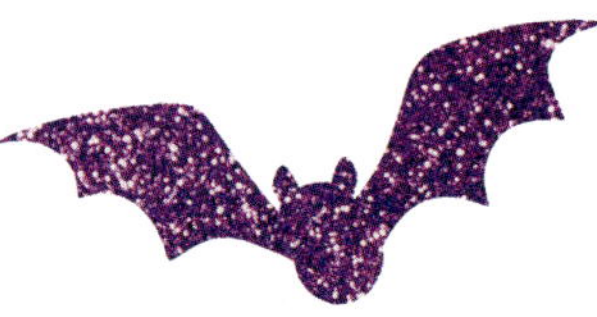

Honey

Cinnamon

Step 6 In a small dish, mix together the honey, cinnamon, and orange zest.

Step 7 Spoon an equal amount of the honey mixture into the hole in each apple. Pour the orange juice into the dish.

Step 8 Bake the apples for about 30 minutes. Remove the apples from the oven and set the dish on a potholder. Spoon the juices over the apples. Then spoon the blackberries over the apples, letting them spill into the dish. Return to the oven for about 15 minutes.

Step 9 Remove the apples from the oven and serve while hot.

Horrifying Rubble

This horrifying rubble, decorated with Halloween candy, is gruesome but delicious. While the oven is full of cupcakes and roasting mummies, get mixing and making this fantastic sweet party dessert.

The quantities on this page will make up to 15 portions.

Ingredients

- 1½ cups of semisweet chocolate (broken into small pieces)
- 1 stick of butter or margarine
- 4 tablespoons of corn syrup
- 4 cups of Rice Krispies
- 1 cup mixed dried fruits
- 2 heaping cups of mini marshmallows
- 1 cup of white chocolate (broken into small pieces)
- Your choice of Halloween candy, including vampire teeth, severed fingers, snakes, gummy worms, and other gruesome, chewy treats

Step 1 Line the baking pan with plastic wrap. Make sure the plastic wrap hangs over the edges of the pan.

Dried cranberries

Dried blueberries

Rice Krispies

Mini marshmallows

Step 2 Add the Rice Krispies, dried fruit, and marshmallows to the mixing bowl.

Syrup

Step 3 Add the semisweet chocolate, butter, and syrup to a saucepan.

Semisweet chocolate

Stick of butter

Equipment

- Rectangular baking pan approximately 12 inches × 8 inches (30 × 20 cm)
- Plastic wrap
- Large mixing bowl
- Wooden spoon
- 2 small saucepans
- Small bowl
- Chopping board and large knife

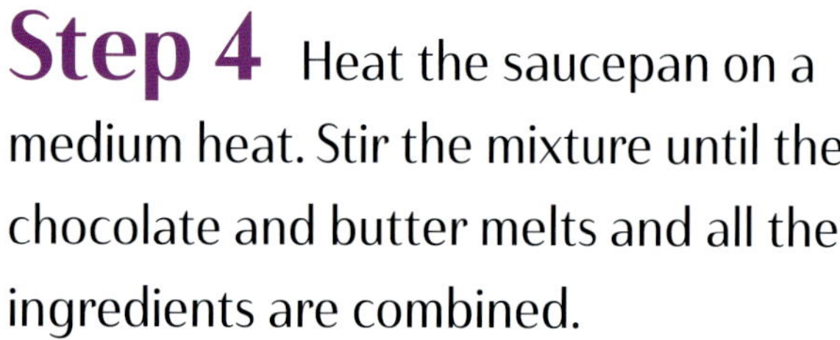

Step 4 Heat the saucepan on a medium heat. Stir the mixture until the chocolate and butter melts and all the ingredients are combined.

Step 5 Pour the melted chocolate mixture into the mixing bowl and gently stir until all the dry ingredients are coated with chocolate.

Step 6 Spoon the mixture into the baking pan and gently press it down.

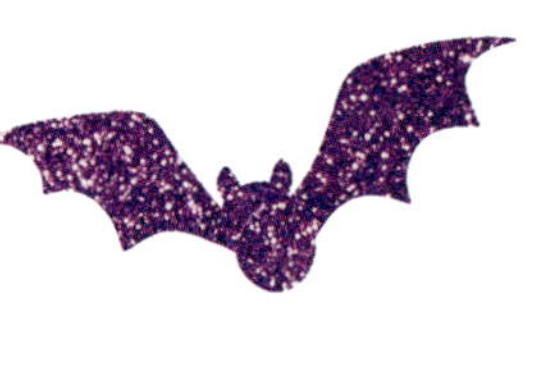

Step 7 Melt the white chocolate pieces using the method described on page 9.

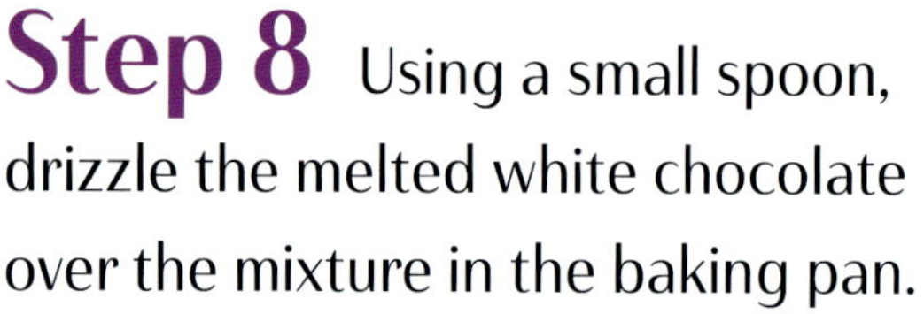

Step 8 Using a small spoon, drizzle the melted white chocolate over the mixture in the baking pan.

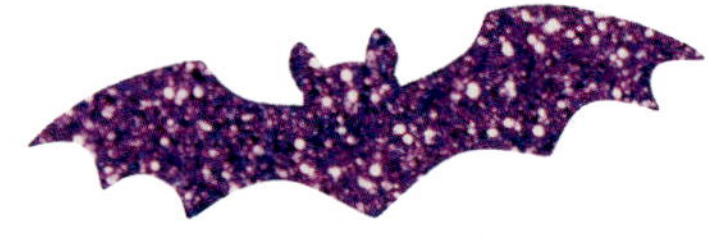

Step 9 Finally, decorate the rubble with Halloween candy and other gory treats. Gently press the candies onto the mixture.

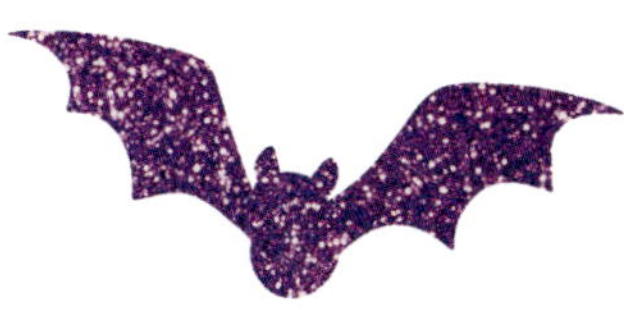

Step 10 Place the pan of rubble mixture into the refrigerator to chill for at least an hour. (Alternatively, make this recipe the day before your Halloween celebrations.)

Step 11 When the rubble has set and is firm, gently lift the plastic wrap and slab of rubble from the pan and place on a cutting board.

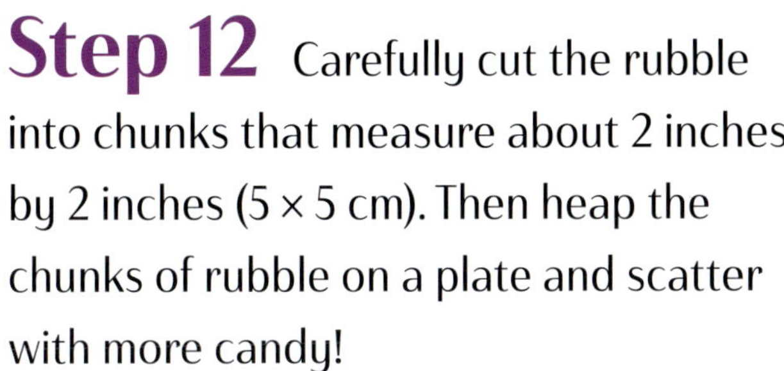

Step 12 Carefully cut the rubble into chunks that measure about 2 inches by 2 inches (5 × 5 cm). Then heap the chunks of rubble on a plate and scatter with more candy!

beat
To blend a mixture of ingredients until they are smooth with equipment such as a spoon, fork, hand whisk, or electric mixer.

consistency
The thickness of a substance. For example, peanut butter has a thick consistency, while milk has a thin consistency.

cream together
To beat butter or margarine, usually with sugar, to make it light and fluffy.

dough
A thick mixture of flour, a liquid such as water or milk, and other ingredients, used for making baked goods such as bread and cookies.

drizzle
To trickle a thin stream of liquid (such as runny frosting or a sauce) over food.

glaze
A liquid that dries and gives an item, such as a cake or cookie, a shiny surface.

knead
To press, squeeze, and fold dough with your hands to make it smooth and stretchy.

perforations
A line of tiny holes or slots in a material that make it easier to tear the material along that line.

preheat
To turn on an oven so it is at the correct temperature for cooking a particular dish before the food is placed inside.

zest
The brightly colored outer part of the rind of citrus fruits, such as lemons and oranges.

Read More

Owen, Ruth. *A Book of Ghoulish Halloween Crafts for Kids Who Dare to Scare (A Kid's Guide to DIY)*. New York: Windmill Books, 2022.

Owen, Ruth. *Kids Throw a Party! (Creative Kids)*. New York: Windmill Books, 2017.

Owen, Ruth. *Let's Celebrate with More Halloween Origami (Let's Celebrate with Origami)*. New York: Enslow Publishers, 2022.

Websites

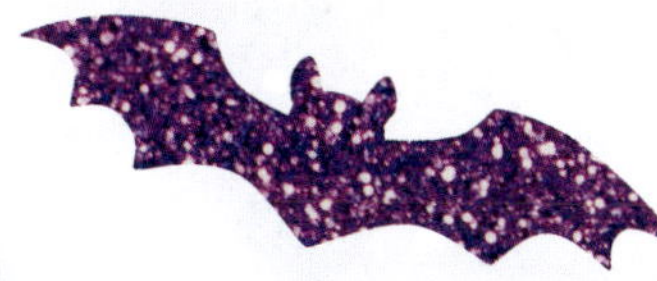

https://kids.nationalgeographic.com/pages/topic/halloween-hangout

https://www.thespruceeats.com/halloween-recipes-for-kids-2098181

https://www.foodnetwork.com/recipes/photos/spooky-halloween-recipes-for-kids

Index